BOOKWORMS

The Making of Everyday Things

Crayons

Derek Miller

Cavendish Square
New York

Published in 2020 by Cavendish Square Publishing, LLC
243 5th Avenue, Suite 136, New York, NY 10016

First Edition

Library of Congress Cataloging-in-Publication Data

Names: Miller, Derek L., author.
Title: Crayons / Derek Miller.
Description: First edition. | New York : Cavendish Square, 2020. | Series: The making of everyday things | Includes bibliographical references and index.
Identifiers: LCCN 2018053415 (print) | LCCN 2018057511 (ebook) | ISBN 9781502646972 (ebook) | ISBN 9781502646965 (library bound) | ISBN 9781502646941 (pbk.) | ISBN 9781502646958 (6 pack)
Subjects: LCSH: Crayons--Juvenile literature. | Paraffin wax--Juvenile literature.
Classification: LCC TS1268 (ebook) | LCC TS1268 .M54 2020 (print) | DDC 665.5/385--dc23
LC record available at https://lccn.loc.gov/2018053415

Editorial Director: David McNamara
Copy Editor: Nathan Heidelberger
Associate Art Director: Alan Sliwinski
Designer: Ginny Kemmerer
Production Coordinator: Karol Szymczuk
Photo Research: J8 Media

The photographs in this book are used by permission and through the courtesy of: Cover, Pao Laroid/Shutterstock.com; p. 5 Stretch Photography/Getty Images; p. 7 Gmhofmann, own work/File: Paraffin.jpg/Wikimedia Commons/CCA-SA 3.0 Unported; p. 9 Dex Image/Getty Images; p. 11 Charles LeRette/Alamy Stock Photo; pp. 13, 17 William Thomas Cain/Getty Images; p. 15 Steve Klaver/AP Images; p. 19 Rick Smith/AP Images; p. 21 Cvm/Shutterstock.com.

Printed in the United States of America

Contents

Crayons come in many colors.

People use crayons to draw.

It takes many steps to make crayons.

Crayons are made from **wax**.

The wax is cool.

It is solid.

The wax is in small pieces.

The wax goes to a **factory**.

This is where crayons
are made.

The wax is heated.

This makes it liquid.

The wax goes into a big **silo**.

The silo is part of the factory.

The wax is still hot.

The wax is still liquid.

Pigment is added.

Pigment is colored **powder**.

It gives the crayons
their color.

The wax and pigment
are mixed.

The **mixture** goes into a mold.

A mold gives something its shape.

The mold is shaped like crayons.

The wax cools.

It turns solid again.

Crayons come out of the mold.

Now it's time for labels.

The label is wrapped twice.

This makes the crayon stronger.

It won't break easily.

TURN TO CRAYON
Crayola
Crayola

Machines move the crayons.

The crayons go into boxes.

The crayons are ready!

New Words

factory (FAK-tuh-ree) A place where things are made.

mixture (MIKS-cher) A blend of two or more things.

powder (POW-der) Something very fine like sand.

silo (SY-lo) A tall building used to store things.

wax (WACKS) A material that can be molded.

Index

About the Author

Derek Miller is a teacher and writer. He likes to learn interesting facts about things we see every day.

About BOOKWORMS

Bookworms help independent readers gain reading confidence through high-frequency words, simple sentences, and strong picture/text support. Each book explores a concept that helps children relate what they read to the world they live in.